Poop Log

A Journal For Your Turds

Douglas Fir

Dragonfly Systems
Portland, Maine

© 2015 by Douglas Fir

ISBN: 978-1517503444

Dedicated to Larry, the guy who works behind the counter at my local fast-food taco joint. You are responsible for the number and quality of the vast majority of my bowel movements. The entire toilet paper and bathroom spray industries owe you an entire debt.

Date: _____ **Time:** _____

Size | Length: _____ **Width:** _____

Texture: _____
_____
_____

Odor: _____
_____
_____

Color: _____

Nuts: _____ **Corn:** _____ **Plastic Toys:** _____ **Other:** _____

Amount of Toilet Paper Used: _____
_____

Amount of time to clear the odor from bathroom: _____
_____

Anyone else in the house disturbed by the smell: _____
_____

Notes: _____
_____
_____

What the hell did you eat: _____

_____

_____

_____

How did you feel after: _____

_____

_____

Draw a doodle of your doodoo:

Date: _____ **Time:** _____

Size | Length: _____ **Width:** _____

Texture: _____

_____

_____

Odor: _____

_____

_____

Color: _____

Nuts: _____ **Corn:** _____ **Plastic Toys:** _____ **Other:** _____

Amount of Toilet Paper Used: _____

_____

Amount of time to clear the odor from bathroom: _____

_____

Anyone else in the house disturbed by the smell: _____

_____

Notes: _____

_____

_____

What the hell did you eat: _____

_____

_____

_____

How did you feel after: _____

_____

_____

Draw a doodle of your doodoo:

Date: _____ **Time:** _____

Size | Length: _____ **Width:** _____

Texture: _____

_____

_____

Odor: _____

_____

_____

Color: _____

Nuts: _____ **Corn:** _____ **Plastic Toys:** _____ **Other:** _____

Amount of Toilet Paper Used: _____

_____

Amount of time to clear the odor from bathroom: _____

_____

Anyone else in the house disturbed by the smell: _____

_____

Notes: _____

_____

_____

What the hell did you eat: _____

_____

_____

_____

How did you feel after: _____

_____

_____

Draw a doodle of your doodoo:

Date: _____ **Time:** _____

Size | Length: _____ **Width:** _____

Texture: _____

_____

_____

Odor: _____

_____

_____

Color: _____

Nuts: _____ **Corn:** _____ **Plastic Toys:** _____ **Other:** _____

Amount of Toilet Paper Used: _____

_____

Amount of time to clear the odor from bathroom: _____

_____

Anyone else in the house disturbed by the smell: _____

_____

Notes: _____

_____

_____

What the hell did you eat: _____

_____

_____

_____

How did you feel after: _____

_____

_____

Draw a doodle of your doodoo:

Date: _____ **Time:** _____

Size | Length: _____ **Width:** _____

Texture: _____

_____

_____

Odor: _____

_____

_____

Color: _____

Nuts: _____ **Corn:** _____ **Plastic Toys:** _____ **Other:** _____

Amount of Toilet Paper Used: _____

_____

Amount of time to clear the odor from bathroom: _____

_____

Anyone else in the house disturbed by the smell: _____

_____

Notes: _____

_____

_____

What the hell did you eat: _____

_____

_____

_____

How did you feel after: _____

_____

_____

Draw a doodle of your doodoo:

Date: _____ **Time:** _____

Size | Length: _____ **Width:** _____

Texture: _____

_____

_____

Odor: _____

_____

_____

Color: _____

Nuts: _____ **Corn:** _____ **Plastic Toys:** _____ **Other:** _____

Amount of Toilet Paper Used: _____

_____

Amount of time to clear the odor from bathroom: _____

_____

Anyone else in the house disturbed by the smell: _____

_____

Notes: _____

_____

_____

What the hell did you eat: _____

_____

_____

_____

How did you feel after: _____

_____

_____

Draw a doodle of your doodoo:

Date: _____ **Time:** _____

Size | Length: _____ **Width:** _____

Texture: _____

_____

_____

Odor: _____

_____

_____

Color: _____

Nuts: _____ **Corn:** _____ **Plastic Toys:** _____ **Other:** _____

Amount of Toilet Paper Used: _____

_____

Amount of time to clear the odor from bathroom: _____

_____

Anyone else in the house disturbed by the smell: _____

_____

Notes: _____

_____

_____

What the hell did you eat: _____

_____

_____

_____

How did you feel after: _____

_____

_____

Draw a doodle of your doodoo:

Date: _____ **Time:** _____

Size | Length: _____ **Width:** _____

Texture: _____

_____

_____

Odor: _____

_____

_____

Color: _____

Nuts: _____ **Corn:** _____ **Plastic Toys:** _____ **Other:** _____

Amount of Toilet Paper Used: _____

_____

Amount of time to clear the odor from bathroom: _____

_____

Anyone else in the house disturbed by the smell: _____

_____

Notes: _____

_____

_____

What the hell did you eat: _____

_____

_____

_____

How did you feel after: _____

_____

_____

Draw a doodle of your doodoo:

Date: _____ **Time:** _____

Size | Length: _____ **Width:** _____

Texture: _____

_____

_____

Odor: _____

_____

_____

Color: _____

Nuts: _____ **Corn:** _____ **Plastic Toys:** _____ **Other:** _____

Amount of Toilet Paper Used: _____

_____

Amount of time to clear the odor from bathroom: _____

_____

Anyone else in the house disturbed by the smell: _____

_____

Notes: _____

_____

_____

What the hell did you eat: _____

_____

_____

_____

How did you feel after: _____

_____

_____

Draw a doodle of your doodoo:

Date: _____ **Time:** _____

Size | Length: _____ **Width:** _____

Texture: _____

_____

_____

Odor: _____

_____

_____

Color: _____

Nuts: _____ **Corn:** _____ **Plastic Toys:** _____ **Other:** _____

Amount of Toilet Paper Used: _____

_____

Amount of time to clear the odor from bathroom: _____

_____

Anyone else in the house disturbed by the smell: _____

_____

Notes: _____

_____

_____

What the hell did you eat: _____

_____

_____

_____

How did you feel after: _____

_____

_____

Draw a doodle of your doodoo:

Date: _____ **Time:** _____

Size | Length: _____ **Width:** _____

Texture: _____

_____

_____

Odor: _____

_____

_____

Color: _____

Nuts: _____ **Corn:** _____ **Plastic Toys:** _____ **Other:** _____

Amount of Toilet Paper Used: _____

_____

Amount of time to clear the odor from bathroom: _____

_____

Anyone else in the house disturbed by the smell: _____

_____

Notes: _____

_____

_____

What the hell did you eat: _____

_____

_____

_____

How did you feel after: _____

_____

_____

Draw a doodle of your doodoo:

Date: _____ **Time:** _____

Size | Length: _____ **Width:** _____

Texture: _____

_____

_____

Odor: _____

_____

_____

Color: _____

Nuts: _____ **Corn:** _____ **Plastic Toys:** _____ **Other:** _____

Amount of Toilet Paper Used: _____

_____

Amount of time to clear the odor from bathroom: _____

_____

Anyone else in the house disturbed by the smell: _____

_____

Notes: _____

_____

_____

What the hell did you eat: _____

_____

_____

_____

How did you feel after: _____

_____

_____

Draw a doodle of your doodoo:

Date: _____ Time: _____

Size | Length: _____ Width: _____

Texture: _____
_____
_____

Odor: _____
_____
_____

Color: _____

Nuts: _____ Corn: _____ Plastic Toys: _____ Other: _____

Amount of Toilet Paper Used: _____
_____

Amount of time to clear the odor from bathroom: _____
_____

Anyone else in the house disturbed by the smell: _____
_____

Notes: _____
_____
_____

What the hell did you eat: _____

_____

_____

_____

How did you feel after: _____

_____

_____

Draw a doodle of your doodoo:

Date: _____ **Time:** _____

Size | Length: _____ **Width:** _____

Texture: _____

_____

_____

Odor: _____

_____

_____

Color: _____

Nuts: _____ **Corn:** _____ **Plastic Toys:** _____ **Other:** _____

Amount of Toilet Paper Used: _____

_____

Amount of time to clear the odor from bathroom: _____

_____

Anyone else in the house disturbed by the smell: _____

_____

Notes: _____

_____

_____

What the hell did you eat: _____

_____

_____

_____

How did you feel after: _____

_____

_____

Draw a doodle of your doodoo:

Date: _____ **Time:** _____

Size | Length: _____ **Width:** _____

Texture: _____
_____
_____

Odor: _____
_____
_____

Color: _____

Nuts: _____ **Corn:** _____ **Plastic Toys:** _____ **Other:** _____

Amount of Toilet Paper Used: _____
_____

Amount of time to clear the odor from bathroom: _____
_____

Anyone else in the house disturbed by the smell: _____
_____

Notes: _____
_____
_____

What the hell did you eat: _____

_____

_____

_____

How did you feel after: _____

_____

_____

Draw a doodle of your doodoo:

Date: _____ **Time:** _____

Size | Length: _____ **Width:** _____

Texture: _____

_____

_____

Odor: _____

_____

_____

Color: _____

Nuts: _____ **Corn:** _____ **Plastic Toys:** _____ **Other:** _____

Amount of Toilet Paper Used: _____

_____

Amount of time to clear the odor from bathroom: _____

_____

Anyone else in the house disturbed by the smell: _____

_____

Notes: _____

_____

_____

What the hell did you eat: _____

_____

_____

_____

How did you feel after: _____

_____

_____

Draw a doodle of your doodoo:

Date: _____ **Time:** _____

Size | Length: _____ **Width:** _____

Texture: _____

_____

_____

Odor: _____

_____

_____

Color: _____

Nuts: _____ **Corn:** _____ **Plastic Toys:** _____ **Other:** _____

Amount of Toilet Paper Used: _____

_____

Amount of time to clear the odor from bathroom: _____

_____

Anyone else in the house disturbed by the smell: _____

_____

Notes: _____

_____

_____

What the hell did you eat: _____

_____

_____

_____

How did you feel after: _____

_____

_____

Draw a doodle of your doodoo:

Date: _____ **Time:** _____

Size | Length: _____ **Width:** _____

Texture: _____

_____

_____

Odor: _____

_____

_____

Color: _____

Nuts: _____ **Corn:** _____ **Plastic Toys:** _____ **Other:** _____

Amount of Toilet Paper Used: _____

_____

Amount of time to clear the odor from bathroom: _____

_____

Anyone else in the house disturbed by the smell: _____

_____

Notes: _____

_____

_____

What the hell did you eat: _____

_____

_____

_____

How did you feel after: _____

_____

_____

Draw a doodle of your doodoo:

Date: _____ **Time:** _____

Size | Length: _____ **Width:** _____

Texture: _____

_____

_____

Odor: _____

_____

_____

Color: _____

Nuts: _____ **Corn:** _____ **Plastic Toys:** _____ **Other:** _____

Amount of Toilet Paper Used: _____

_____

Amount of time to clear the odor from bathroom: _____

_____

Anyone else in the house disturbed by the smell: _____

_____

Notes: _____

_____

_____

What the hell did you eat: _____

_____

_____

_____

How did you feel after: _____

_____

_____

Draw a doodle of your doodoo:

Date: _____ **Time:** _____

Size | Length: _____ **Width:** _____

Texture: _____

_____

_____

Odor: _____

_____

_____

Color: _____

Nuts: _____ **Corn:** _____ **Plastic Toys:** _____ **Other:** _____

Amount of Toilet Paper Used: _____

_____

Amount of time to clear the odor from bathroom: _____

_____

Anyone else in the house disturbed by the smell: _____

_____

Notes: _____

_____

_____

What the hell did you eat: _____

_____

_____

_____

How did you feel after: _____

_____

_____

Draw a doodle of your doodoo:

Date: _____ **Time:** _____

Size | Length: _____ **Width:** _____

Texture: _____

_____

_____

Odor: _____

_____

_____

Color: _____

Nuts: _____ **Corn:** _____ **Plastic Toys:** _____ **Other:** _____

Amount of Toilet Paper Used: _____

_____

Amount of time to clear the odor from bathroom: _____

_____

Anyone else in the house disturbed by the smell: _____

_____

Notes: _____

_____

_____

What the hell did you eat: _____

_____

_____

_____

How did you feel after: _____

_____

_____

Draw a doodle of your doodoo:

Date: _____ **Time:** _____

Size | Length: _____ **Width:** _____

Texture: _____

_____

_____

Odor: _____

_____

_____

Color: _____

Nuts: _____ **Corn:** _____ **Plastic Toys:** _____ **Other:** _____

Amount of Toilet Paper Used: _____

_____

Amount of time to clear the odor from bathroom: _____

_____

Anyone else in the house disturbed by the smell: _____

_____

Notes: _____

_____

_____

What the hell did you eat: _____

_____

_____

_____

How did you feel after: _____

_____

_____

Draw a doodle of your doodoo:

Date: _____ Time: _____

Size | Length: _____ Width: _____

Texture: _____
_____
_____

Odor: _____
_____
_____

Color: _____

Nuts: _____ Corn: _____ Plastic Toys: _____ Other: _____

Amount of Toilet Paper Used: _____
_____

Amount of time to clear the odor from bathroom: _____
_____

Anyone else in the house disturbed by the smell: _____
_____

Notes: _____
_____
_____

What the hell did you eat: _____

_____

_____

_____

How did you feel after: _____

_____

_____

Draw a doodle of your doodoo:

Date: _____ Time: _____

Size | Length: _____ Width: _____

Texture: _____

_____

_____

Odor: _____

_____

_____

Color: _____

Nuts: _____ Corn: _____ Plastic Toys: _____ Other: _____

Amount of Toilet Paper Used: _____

_____

Amount of time to clear the odor from bathroom: _____

_____

Anyone else in the house disturbed by the smell: _____

_____

Notes: _____

_____

_____

What the hell did you eat: _____

_____

_____

_____

How did you feel after: _____

_____

_____

Draw a doodle of your doodoo:

Date: _____ **Time:** _____

Size | Length: _____ **Width:** _____

Texture: _____

_____

_____

Odor: _____

_____

_____

Color: _____

Nuts: _____ **Corn:** _____ **Plastic Toys:** _____ **Other:** _____

Amount of Toilet Paper Used: _____

_____

Amount of time to clear the odor from bathroom: _____

_____

Anyone else in the house disturbed by the smell: _____

_____

Notes: _____

_____

_____

What the hell did you eat: _____

_____

_____

_____

How did you feel after: _____

_____

_____

Draw a doodle of your doodoo:

Date: _____ **Time:** _____

Size | Length: _____ **Width:** _____

Texture: _____

_____

_____

Odor: _____

_____

_____

Color: _____

Nuts: _____ **Corn:** _____ **Plastic Toys:** _____ **Other:** _____

Amount of Toilet Paper Used: _____

_____

Amount of time to clear the odor from bathroom: _____

_____

Anyone else in the house disturbed by the smell: _____

_____

Notes: _____

_____

_____

What the hell did you eat: _____

_____

_____

_____

How did you feel after: _____

_____

_____

Draw a doodle of your doodoo:

Date: _____ **Time:** _____

Size | Length: _____ **Width:** _____

Texture: _____

_____

_____

Odor: _____

_____

_____

Color: _____

Nuts: _____ **Corn:** _____ **Plastic Toys:** _____ **Other:** _____

Amount of Toilet Paper Used: _____

_____

Amount of time to clear the odor from bathroom: _____

_____

Anyone else in the house disturbed by the smell: _____

_____

Notes: _____

_____

_____

What the hell did you eat: _____

_____

_____

_____

How did you feel after: _____

_____

_____

Draw a doodle of your doodoo:

Date: _____ Time: _____

Size | Length: _____ Width: _____

Texture: _____
_____
_____

Odor: _____
_____
_____

Color: _____

Nuts: _____ Corn: _____ Plastic Toys: _____ Other: _____

Amount of Toilet Paper Used: _____
_____

Amount of time to clear the odor from bathroom: _____
_____

Anyone else in the house disturbed by the smell: _____
_____

Notes: _____
_____
_____

What the hell did you eat: _____

_____

_____

_____

How did you feel after: _____

_____

_____

Draw a doodle of your doodoo:

_____

Date: _____ **Time:** _____

Size | Length: _____ **Width:** _____

Texture: _____

_____

_____

Odor: _____

_____

_____

Color: _____

Nuts: _____ **Corn:** _____ **Plastic Toys:** _____ **Other:** _____

Amount of Toilet Paper Used: _____

_____

Amount of time to clear the odor from bathroom: _____

_____

Anyone else in the house disturbed by the smell: _____

_____

Notes: _____

_____

_____

What the hell did you eat: _____

_____

_____

_____

How did you feel after: _____

_____

_____

Draw a doodle of your doodoo:

Date: _____ **Time:** _____

Size | Length: _____ **Width:** _____

Texture: _____

_____

_____

Odor: _____

_____

_____

Color: _____

Nuts: _____ **Corn:** _____ **Plastic Toys:** _____ **Other:** _____

Amount of Toilet Paper Used: _____

_____

Amount of time to clear the odor from bathroom: _____

_____

Anyone else in the house disturbed by the smell: _____

_____

Notes: _____

_____

_____

What the hell did you eat: _____

_____

_____

_____

How did you feel after: _____

_____

_____

Draw a doodle of your doodoo:

Date: _____ Time: _____

Size | Length: _____ Width: _____

Texture: _____
_____
_____

Odor: _____
_____
_____

Color: _____

Nuts: _____ Corn: _____ Plastic Toys: _____ Other: _____

Amount of Toilet Paper Used: _____
_____

Amount of time to clear the odor from bathroom: _____
_____

Anyone else in the house disturbed by the smell: _____
_____

Notes: _____
_____
_____

What the hell did you eat: _____

_____

_____

_____

How did you feel after: _____

_____

_____

Draw a doodle of your doodoo:

Date: _____ **Time:** _____

Size | Length: _____ **Width:** _____

Texture: _____

_____

_____

Odor: _____

_____

_____

Color: _____

Nuts: _____ **Corn:** _____ **Plastic Toys:** _____ **Other:** _____

Amount of Toilet Paper Used: _____

_____

Amount of time to clear the odor from bathroom: _____

_____

Anyone else in the house disturbed by the smell: _____

_____

Notes: _____

_____

_____

What the hell did you eat: _____

_____

_____

_____

How did you feel after: _____

_____

_____

Draw a doodle of your doodoo:

Date: _____ **Time:** _____

Size | Length: _____ **Width:** _____

Texture: _____

_____

_____

Odor: _____

_____

_____

Color: _____

Nuts: _____ **Corn:** _____ **Plastic Toys:** _____ **Other:** _____

Amount of Toilet Paper Used: _____

_____

Amount of time to clear the odor from bathroom: _____

_____

Anyone else in the house disturbed by the smell: _____

_____

Notes: _____

_____

_____

What the hell did you eat: _____

_____

_____

_____

How did you feel after: _____

_____

_____

Draw a doodle of your doodoo:

Date: _____ **Time:** _____

Size | Length: _____ **Width:** _____

Texture: _____

_____

_____

Odor: _____

_____

_____

Color: _____

Nuts: _____ **Corn:** _____ **Plastic Toys:** _____ **Other:** _____

Amount of Toilet Paper Used: _____

_____

Amount of time to clear the odor from bathroom: _____

_____

Anyone else in the house disturbed by the smell: _____

_____

Notes: _____

_____

_____

What the hell did you eat: _____

_____

_____

_____

How did you feel after: _____

_____

_____

Draw a doodle of your doodoo:

Date: _____ Time: _____

Size | Length: _____ Width: _____

Texture: _____
_____
_____

Odor: _____
_____
_____

Color: _____

Nuts: _____ Corn: _____ Plastic Toys: _____ Other: _____

Amount of Toilet Paper Used: _____
_____

Amount of time to clear the odor from bathroom: _____
_____

Anyone else in the house disturbed by the smell: _____
_____

Notes: _____
_____
_____

What the hell did you eat: _____

_____

_____

_____

How did you feel after: _____

_____

_____

Draw a doodle of your doodoo:

Date: _____ **Time:** _____

Size | Length: _____ **Width:** _____

Texture: _____

_____

_____

Odor: _____

_____

_____

Color: _____

Nuts: _____ **Corn:** _____ **Plastic Toys:** _____ **Other:** _____

Amount of Toilet Paper Used: _____

_____

Amount of time to clear the odor from bathroom: _____

_____

Anyone else in the house disturbed by the smell: _____

_____

Notes: _____

_____

_____

What the hell did you eat: _____

_____

_____

_____

How did you feel after: _____

_____

_____

Draw a doodle of your doodoo:

Date: _____ **Time:** _____

Size | Length: _____ **Width:** _____

Texture: _____

_____

_____

Odor: _____

_____

_____

Color: _____

Nuts: _____ **Corn:** _____ **Plastic Toys:** _____ **Other:** _____

Amount of Toilet Paper Used: _____

_____

Amount of time to clear the odor from bathroom: _____

_____

Anyone else in the house disturbed by the smell: _____

_____

Notes: _____

_____

_____

What the hell did you eat: _____

_____

_____

_____

How did you feel after: _____

_____

_____

Draw a doodle of your doodoo:

Date: _____ **Time:** _____

Size | Length: _____ **Width:** _____

Texture: _____

_____

_____

Odor: _____

_____

_____

Color: _____

Nuts: _____ **Corn:** _____ **Plastic Toys:** _____ **Other:** _____

Amount of Toilet Paper Used: _____

_____

Amount of time to clear the odor from bathroom: _____

_____

Anyone else in the house disturbed by the smell: _____

_____

Notes: _____

_____

_____

What the hell did you eat: _____

_____

_____

_____

How did you feel after: _____

_____

_____

Draw a doodle of your doodoo:

Date: _____ **Time:** _____

Size | Length: _____ **Width:** _____

Texture: _____

_____

_____

Odor: _____

_____

_____

Color: _____

Nuts: _____ **Corn:** _____ **Plastic Toys:** _____ **Other:** _____

Amount of Toilet Paper Used: _____

_____

Amount of time to clear the odor from bathroom: _____

_____

Anyone else in the house disturbed by the smell: _____

_____

Notes: _____

_____

_____

What the hell did you eat: _____

_____

_____

_____

How did you feel after: _____

_____

_____

Draw a doodle of your doodoo:

Date: _____ **Time:** _____

Size | Length: _____ **Width:** _____

Texture: _____

_____

_____

Odor: _____

_____

_____

Color: _____

Nuts: _____ **Corn:** _____ **Plastic Toys:** _____ **Other:** _____

Amount of Toilet Paper Used: _____

_____

Amount of time to clear the odor from bathroom: _____

_____

Anyone else in the house disturbed by the smell: _____

_____

Notes: _____

_____

_____

What the hell did you eat: _____

_____

_____

How did you feel after: _____

_____

_____

Draw a doodle of your doodoo:

Date: _____ Time: _____

Size | Length: _____ Width: _____

Texture: _____
_____
_____

Odor: _____
_____
_____

Color: _____

Nuts: _____ Corn: _____ Plastic Toys: _____ Other: _____

Amount of Toilet Paper Used: _____
_____

Amount of time to clear the odor from bathroom: _____
_____

Anyone else in the house disturbed by the smell: _____
_____

Notes: _____
_____
_____

What the hell did you eat: _____

_____

_____

How did you feel after: _____

_____

_____

Draw a doodle of your doodoo:

Date: _____ **Time:** _____

Size | Length: _____ **Width:** _____

Texture: _____

_____

_____

Odor: _____

_____

_____

Color: _____

Nuts: _____ **Corn:** _____ **Plastic Toys:** _____ **Other:** _____

Amount of Toilet Paper Used: _____

_____

Amount of time to clear the odor from bathroom: _____

_____

Anyone else in the house disturbed by the smell: _____

_____

Notes: _____

_____

_____

What the hell did you eat: _____

_____

_____

_____

How did you feel after: _____

_____

_____

Draw a doodle of your doodoo:

Date: _____ **Time:** _____

Size | Length: _____ **Width:** _____

Texture: _____

_____

_____

Odor: _____

_____

_____

Color: _____

Nuts: _____ **Corn:** _____ **Plastic Toys:** _____ **Other:** _____

Amount of Toilet Paper Used: _____

_____

Amount of time to clear the odor from bathroom: _____

_____

Anyone else in the house disturbed by the smell: _____

_____

Notes: _____

_____

_____

What the hell did you eat: _____

_____

_____

_____

How did you feel after: _____

_____

_____

Draw a doodle of your doodoo:

Date: _____ **Time:** _____

Size | Length: _____ **Width:** _____

Texture: _____

_____

_____

Odor: _____

_____

_____

Color: _____

Nuts: _____ **Corn:** _____ **Plastic Toys:** _____ **Other:** _____

Amount of Toilet Paper Used: _____

_____

Amount of time to clear the odor from bathroom: _____

_____

Anyone else in the house disturbed by the smell: _____

_____

Notes: _____

_____

_____

What the hell did you eat: _____

_____

_____

_____

How did you feel after: _____

_____

_____

Draw a doodle of your doodoo:

Date: _____ Time: _____

Size | Length: _____ Width: _____

Texture: _____
_____
_____

Odor: _____
_____
_____

Color: _____

Nuts: _____ Corn: _____ Plastic Toys: _____ Other: _____

Amount of Toilet Paper Used: _____
_____

Amount of time to clear the odor from bathroom: _____
_____

Anyone else in the house disturbed by the smell: _____
_____

Notes: _____
_____
_____

What the hell did you eat: _____

_____

_____

_____

How did you feel after: _____

_____

_____

Draw a doodle of your doodoo:

Date: _____ **Time:** _____

Size | Length: _____ **Width:** _____

Texture: _____

_____

_____

Odor: _____

_____

_____

Color: _____

Nuts: _____ **Corn:** _____ **Plastic Toys:** _____ **Other:** _____

Amount of Toilet Paper Used: _____

_____

Amount of time to clear the odor from bathroom: _____

_____

Anyone else in the house disturbed by the smell: _____

_____

Notes: _____

_____

_____

What the hell did you eat: _____

_____

_____

_____

How did you feel after: _____

_____

_____

Draw a doodle of your doodoo:

Date: _____ **Time:** _____

Size | Length: _____ **Width:** _____

Texture: _____

_____

_____

Odor: _____

_____

_____

Color: _____

Nuts: _____ **Corn:** _____ **Plastic Toys:** _____ **Other:** _____

Amount of Toilet Paper Used: _____

_____

Amount of time to clear the odor from bathroom: _____

_____

Anyone else in the house disturbed by the smell: _____

_____

Notes: _____

_____

_____

What the hell did you eat: _____

_____

_____

_____

How did you feel after: _____

_____

_____

Draw a doodle of your doodoo:

Date: _____ **Time:** _____

Size | Length: _____ **Width:** _____

Texture: _____

_____

_____

Odor: _____

_____

_____

Color: _____

Nuts: _____ **Corn:** _____ **Plastic Toys:** _____ **Other:** _____

Amount of Toilet Paper Used: _____

_____

Amount of time to clear the odor from bathroom: _____

_____

Anyone else in the house disturbed by the smell: _____

_____

Notes: _____

_____

_____

What the hell did you eat: _____

_____

_____

_____

How did you feel after: _____

_____

_____

Draw a doodle of your doodoo:

Date: _____ **Time:** _____

Size | Length: _____ **Width:** _____

Texture: _____

_____

_____

Odor: _____

_____

_____

Color: _____

Nuts: _____ **Corn:** _____ **Plastic Toys:** _____ **Other:** _____

Amount of Toilet Paper Used: _____

_____

Amount of time to clear the odor from bathroom: _____

_____

Anyone else in the house disturbed by the smell: _____

_____

Notes: _____

_____

_____

What the hell did you eat: _____

_____

_____

_____

How did you feel after: _____

_____

_____

Draw a doodle of your doodoo:

Date: _____ **Time:** _____

Size | Length: _____ **Width:** _____

Texture: _____

_____

_____

Odor: _____

_____

_____

Color: _____

Nuts: _____ **Corn:** _____ **Plastic Toys:** _____ **Other:** _____

Amount of Toilet Paper Used: _____

_____

Amount of time to clear the odor from bathroom: _____

_____

Anyone else in the house disturbed by the smell: _____

_____

Notes: _____

_____

_____

What the hell did you eat: _____

_____

_____

_____

How did you feel after: _____

_____

_____

Draw a doodle of your doodoo:

Date: _____ **Time:** _____

Size | Length: _____ **Width:** _____

Texture: _____

_____

_____

Odor: _____

_____

_____

Color: _____

Nuts: _____ **Corn:** _____ **Plastic Toys:** _____ **Other:** _____

Amount of Toilet Paper Used: _____

_____

Amount of time to clear the odor from bathroom: _____

_____

Anyone else in the house disturbed by the smell: _____

_____

Notes: _____

_____

_____

What the hell did you eat: _____

_____

_____

_____

How did you feel after: _____

_____

_____

Draw a doodle of your doodoo:

Date: _____ **Time:** _____

Size | Length: _____ **Width:** _____

Texture: _____
_____
_____

Odor: _____
_____
_____

Color: _____

Nuts: _____ **Corn:** _____ **Plastic Toys:** _____ **Other:** _____

Amount of Toilet Paper Used: _____
_____

Amount of time to clear the odor from bathroom: _____
_____

Anyone else in the house disturbed by the smell: _____
_____

Notes: _____
_____
_____

What the hell did you eat: _____

_____

_____

_____

How did you feel after: _____

_____

_____

Draw a doodle of your doodoo:

Date: _____ **Time:** _____

Size | Length: _____ **Width:** _____

Texture: _____

_____

_____

Odor: _____

_____

_____

Color: _____

Nuts: _____ **Corn:** _____ **Plastic Toys:** _____ **Other:** _____

Amount of Toilet Paper Used: _____

_____

Amount of time to clear the odor from bathroom: _____

_____

Anyone else in the house disturbed by the smell: _____

_____

Notes: _____

_____

_____

What the hell did you eat: _____

_____

_____

_____

How did you feel after: _____

_____

_____

Draw a doodle of your doodoo:

Date: _____ **Time:** _____

Size | Length: _____ **Width:** _____

Texture: _____

_____

_____

Odor: _____

_____

_____

Color: _____

Nuts: _____ **Corn:** _____ **Plastic Toys:** _____ **Other:** _____

Amount of Toilet Paper Used: _____

_____

Amount of time to clear the odor from bathroom: _____

_____

Anyone else in the house disturbed by the smell: _____

_____

Notes: _____

_____

_____

What the hell did you eat: _____

_____

_____

_____

How did you feel after: _____

_____

_____

Draw a doodle of your doodoo:

Date: _____ **Time:** _____

Size | Length: _____ **Width:** _____

Texture: _____

_____

_____

Odor: _____

_____

_____

Color: _____

Nuts: _____ **Corn:** _____ **Plastic Toys:** _____ **Other:** _____

Amount of Toilet Paper Used: _____

_____

Amount of time to clear the odor from bathroom: _____

_____

Anyone else in the house disturbed by the smell: _____

_____

Notes: _____

_____

_____

What the hell did you eat: _____

_____

_____

_____

How did you feel after: _____

_____

_____

Draw a doodle of your doodoo:

Date: _____ **Time:** _____

Size | Length: _____ **Width:** _____

Texture: _____

_____

_____

Odor: _____

_____

_____

Color: _____

Nuts: _____ **Corn:** _____ **Plastic Toys:** _____ **Other:** _____

Amount of Toilet Paper Used: _____

_____

Amount of time to clear the odor from bathroom: _____

_____

Anyone else in the house disturbed by the smell: _____

_____

Notes: _____

_____

_____

What the hell did you eat: _____

_____

_____

_____

How did you feel after: _____

_____

_____

Draw a doodle of your doodoo:

Date: _____ **Time:** _____

Size | Length: _____ **Width:** _____

Texture: _____

_____

_____

Odor: _____

_____

_____

Color: _____

Nuts: _____ **Corn:** _____ **Plastic Toys:** _____ **Other:** _____

Amount of Toilet Paper Used: _____

_____

Amount of time to clear the odor from bathroom: _____

_____

Anyone else in the house disturbed by the smell: _____

_____

Notes: _____

_____

_____

What the hell did you eat: _____

_____

_____

_____

How did you feel after: _____

_____

_____

Draw a doodle of your doodoo:

Date: _____ **Time:** _____

Size | Length: _____ **Width:** _____

Texture: _____

_____

_____

Odor: _____

_____

_____

Color: _____

Nuts: _____ **Corn:** _____ **Plastic Toys:** _____ **Other:** _____

Amount of Toilet Paper Used: _____

_____

Amount of time to clear the odor from bathroom: _____

_____

Anyone else in the house disturbed by the smell: _____

_____

Notes: _____

_____

_____

What the hell did you eat: _____

_____

_____

_____

How did you feel after: _____

_____

_____

Draw a doodle of your doodoo:

Date: _____ **Time:** _____

Size | Length: _____ **Width:** _____

Texture: _____

_____

_____

Odor: _____

_____

_____

Color: _____

Nuts: _____ **Corn:** _____ **Plastic Toys:** _____ **Other:** _____

Amount of Toilet Paper Used: _____

_____

Amount of time to clear the odor from bathroom: _____

_____

Anyone else in the house disturbed by the smell: _____

_____

Notes: _____

_____

_____

What the hell did you eat: _____

_____

_____

_____

How did you feel after: _____

_____

_____

Draw a doodle of your doodoo:

Date: _____ **Time:** _____

Size | Length: _____ **Width:** _____

Texture: _____

_____

_____

Odor: _____

_____

_____

Color: _____

Nuts: _____ **Corn:** _____ **Plastic Toys:** _____ **Other:** _____

Amount of Toilet Paper Used: _____

_____

Amount of time to clear the odor from bathroom: _____

_____

Anyone else in the house disturbed by the smell: _____

_____

Notes: _____

_____

_____

What the hell did you eat: _____

_____

_____

_____

How did you feel after: _____

_____

_____

Draw a doodle of your doodoo:

Date: _____ **Time:** _____

Size | Length: _____ **Width:** _____

Texture: _____

_____

_____

Odor: _____

_____

_____

Color: _____

Nuts: _____ **Corn:** _____ **Plastic Toys:** _____ **Other:** _____

Amount of Toilet Paper Used: _____

_____

Amount of time to clear the odor from bathroom: _____

_____

Anyone else in the house disturbed by the smell: _____

_____

Notes: _____

_____

_____

What the hell did you eat: _____

_____

_____

_____

How did you feel after: _____

_____

_____

Draw a doodle of your doodoo:

Date: _____ **Time:** _____

Size | Length: _____ **Width:** _____

Texture: _____

_____

_____

Odor: _____

_____

_____

Color: _____

Nuts: _____ **Corn:** _____ **Plastic Toys:** _____ **Other:** _____

Amount of Toilet Paper Used: _____

_____

Amount of time to clear the odor from bathroom: _____

_____

Anyone else in the house disturbed by the smell: _____

_____

Notes: _____

_____

_____

What the hell did you eat: _____

_____

_____

_____

How did you feel after: _____

_____

_____

Draw a doodle of your doodoo:

Date: _____ Time: _____

Size | Length: _____ Width: _____

Texture: _____
_____
_____

Odor: _____
_____
_____

Color: _____

Nuts: _____ Corn: _____ Plastic Toys: _____ Other: _____

Amount of Toilet Paper Used: _____
_____

Amount of time to clear the odor from bathroom: _____
_____

Anyone else in the house disturbed by the smell: _____
_____

Notes: _____
_____
_____

What the hell did you eat: _____

_____

_____

_____

How did you feel after: _____

_____

_____

Draw a doodle of your doodoo:

Date: _____ **Time:** _____

Size | Length: _____ **Width:** _____

Texture: _____

_____

_____

Odor: _____

_____

_____

Color: _____

Nuts: _____ **Corn:** _____ **Plastic Toys:** _____ **Other:** _____

Amount of Toilet Paper Used: _____

_____

Amount of time to clear the odor from bathroom: _____

_____

Anyone else in the house disturbed by the smell: _____

_____

Notes: _____

_____

_____

What the hell did you eat: _____

_____

_____

_____

How did you feel after: _____

_____

_____

Draw a doodle of your doodoo:

Date: _____ **Time:** _____

Size | Length: _____ **Width:** _____

Texture: _____

_____

_____

Odor: _____

_____

_____

Color: _____

Nuts: _____ **Corn:** _____ **Plastic Toys:** _____ **Other:** _____

Amount of Toilet Paper Used: _____

_____

Amount of time to clear the odor from bathroom: _____

_____

Anyone else in the house disturbed by the smell: _____

_____

Notes: _____

_____

_____

What the hell did you eat: _____

_____

_____

_____

How did you feel after: _____

_____

_____

Draw a doodle of your doodoo:

Date: _____ **Time:** _____

Size | Length: _____ **Width:** _____

Texture: _____

_____

_____

Odor: _____

_____

_____

Color: _____

Nuts: _____ **Corn:** _____ **Plastic Toys:** _____ **Other:** _____

Amount of Toilet Paper Used: _____

_____

Amount of time to clear the odor from bathroom: _____

_____

Anyone else in the house disturbed by the smell: _____

_____

Notes: _____

_____

_____

What the hell did you eat: _____

_____

_____

_____

How did you feel after: _____

_____

_____

Draw a doodle of your doodoo:

Date: _____ **Time:** _____

Size | Length: _____ **Width:** _____

Texture: _____

_____

_____

Odor: _____

_____

_____

Color: _____

Nuts: _____ **Corn:** _____ **Plastic Toys:** _____ **Other:** _____

Amount of Toilet Paper Used: _____

_____

Amount of time to clear the odor from bathroom: _____

_____

Anyone else in the house disturbed by the smell: _____

_____

Notes: _____

_____

_____

What the hell did you eat: _____

_____

_____

_____

How did you feel after: _____

_____

_____

Draw a doodle of your doodoo:

Date: _____ **Time:** _____

Size | Length: _____ **Width:** _____

Texture: _____

_____

_____

Odor: _____

_____

_____

Color: _____

Nuts: _____ **Corn:** _____ **Plastic Toys:** _____ **Other:** _____

Amount of Toilet Paper Used: _____

_____

Amount of time to clear the odor from bathroom: _____

_____

Anyone else in the house disturbed by the smell: _____

_____

Notes: _____

_____

_____

What the hell did you eat: _____

_____

_____

_____

How did you feel after: _____

_____

_____

Draw a doodle of your doodoo:

Date: _____ **Time:** _____

Size | Length: _____ **Width:** _____

Texture: _____

_____

_____

Odor: _____

_____

_____

Color: _____

Nuts: _____ **Corn:** _____ **Plastic Toys:** _____ **Other:** _____

Amount of Toilet Paper Used: _____

_____

Amount of time to clear the odor from bathroom: _____

_____

Anyone else in the house disturbed by the smell: _____

_____

Notes: _____

_____

_____

What the hell did you eat: _____

_____

_____

_____

How did you feel after: _____

_____

_____

Draw a doodle of your doodoo:

Date: _____ Time: _____

Size | Length: _____ Width: _____

Texture: _____

_____

_____

Odor: _____

_____

_____

Color: _____

Nuts: _____ Corn: _____ Plastic Toys: _____ Other: _____

Amount of Toilet Paper Used: _____

_____

Amount of time to clear the odor from bathroom: _____

_____

Anyone else in the house disturbed by the smell: _____

_____

Notes: _____

_____

_____

What the hell did you eat: _____

_____

_____

_____

How did you feel after: _____

_____

_____

Draw a doodle of your doodoo:

Date: _____ **Time:** _____

Size | Length: _____ **Width:** _____

Texture: _____

_____

_____

Odor: _____

_____

_____

Color: _____

Nuts: _____ **Corn:** _____ **Plastic Toys:** _____ **Other:** _____

Amount of Toilet Paper Used: _____

_____

Amount of time to clear the odor from bathroom: _____

_____

Anyone else in the house disturbed by the smell: _____

_____

Notes: _____

_____

_____

What the hell did you eat: _____

_____

_____

_____

How did you feel after: _____

_____

_____

Draw a doodle of your doodoo:

Date: _____ **Time:** _____

Size | Length: _____ **Width:** _____

Texture: _____

_____

_____

Odor: _____

_____

_____

Color: _____

Nuts: _____ **Corn:** _____ **Plastic Toys:** _____ **Other:** _____

Amount of Toilet Paper Used: _____

_____

Amount of time to clear the odor from bathroom: _____

_____

Anyone else in the house disturbed by the smell: _____

_____

Notes: _____

_____

_____

What the hell did you eat: _____

_____

_____

_____

How did you feel after: _____

_____

_____

Draw a doodle of your doodoo:

Date: _____ **Time:** _____

Size | Length: _____ **Width:** _____

Texture: _____

_____

_____

Odor: _____

_____

_____

Color: _____

Nuts: _____ **Corn:** _____ **Plastic Toys:** _____ **Other:** _____

Amount of Toilet Paper Used: _____

_____

Amount of time to clear the odor from bathroom: _____

_____

Anyone else in the house disturbed by the smell: _____

_____

Notes: _____

_____

_____

What the hell did you eat: _____

_____

_____

_____

How did you feel after: _____

_____

_____

Draw a doodle of your doodoo:

Date: _____ **Time:** _____

Size | Length: _____ **Width:** _____

Texture: _____

_____

_____

Odor: _____

_____

_____

Color: _____

Nuts: _____ **Corn:** _____ **Plastic Toys:** _____ **Other:** _____

Amount of Toilet Paper Used: _____

_____

Amount of time to clear the odor from bathroom: _____

_____

Anyone else in the house disturbed by the smell: _____

_____

Notes: _____

_____

_____

What the hell did you eat: _____

_____

_____

How did you feel after: _____

_____

_____

Draw a doodle of your doodoo:

Made in the USA
Monee, IL
17 April 2022

94927572R00085